MW01166930

WOMEN WHO SOAR

cx80

An Anthology of Stories

Paulette Harper

Thy Word Publishing
California

Women Who Soar is a work of nonfiction.

Interior design by Marsha Malcolm
Editor: Paulette Nunlee

Women Who Soar
© 2018 Paulette Harper
Published by Thy Word Publishing
Antioch, CA 94531
LCCN # 2018911989

Cataloging-in-Publication Data
ISBN- 10:0-692-04214-8
ISBN-13: 978-0-692-04214-4

Contents

INTRODUCTION   5

SOARING THROUGH ADVERSITIES   7

Paulette Harper

SOARING INTO PURPOSE   19

Dr. Elaine Gattis

UNSHAKABLE FAITH   29

Katrina Shaw

MY LIFE REBOOT   41

Roni J. Teson

TEARS FOR MY SISTER   53

Marcy Thomas

FLYING ABOVE THE STORM   67

Shurvone Wright

A CROWN OF BEAUTY   81

Meiah Shaun

INTRODUCTION

Ever since I started writing, I've always loved helping authors, whether by offering coaching, promoting their book or holding writing workshops. The publication of the anthology *Women Who Soar* is no different.

My passion when doing this anthology was to create a platform for women who believed they had a story to share. These seven women answered the call. Each of their stories is unique, yet they all have one thing in common – they have all been tested by life's problems, challenges and struggles, but have come out stronger to establish themselves as trailblazers in their own right.

This anthology, or some call it a book collaboration, shares stories of hope, with each woman outlining certain parts of her life that took her on a journey of transformation.

Candid and touching, each entry shares the writer's own experiences while trying to maneuver through the highs and lows of life.

There is a gamut of stories throughout the pages of *Women Who Soar*. Some women choose to write about the pain of divorce, depression and cancer, and even death. Others share stories of career changes and offer spiritual encouragement.

While writing stories like these, each woman became vulnerable to past experiences, hurts and even the fear of pulling some painful memories from the past. Yet, it's through stories like these that dreams are birthed, purpose is discovered, and women learn to walk in their own power.

Women Who Soar will encourage women to never give up, no matter the circumstances. These women have decided to rise above it all. They have dispelled lies, overcome difficult challenges and are now soaring and doing great works.

Women Who Soar shares the stories of these powerhouse women—leaders, entrepreneurs, pastor's wives, ministers, pastors, visionaries, speakers, life coaches, authors, professionals, mothers, sisters—and their fight against all odds.

Are you ready to take the journey with us? Buckle your seatbelt, as you are about to read how these women are soaring high while living in their purpose.

Paulette Harper
Co-Author

SOARING THROUGH ADVERSITIES

෴

Paulette Harper

"But they that wait upon the Lord shall renew their strength. They shall mount up with wings like eagles; they shall run and not be weary; they shall walk and not faint."

Isaiah 40:31 (TLB)

The dictionary describes *soar* as the ability to rise or aspire to a higher or more exalted level. Sometimes life takes you by surprise: sometimes life throws you unexpected blows and you learn to bounce back from that which came to trip you up or cause you to stumble. It's so easy to allow life to keep us stuck and nonproductive, especially when the blows come one right after another. Life can be so cruel, relationships can end, family and friends come and go, trials and tests seem to never end, and at times we find ourselves looking in the mirror and asking ourselves... how did I get here? I remember asking myself that question so many times.

Unfortunately, as women, we face so many ups and downs, highs and lows, and twists and turns that sometimes make you want to scream STOP!

I had gone through a very rough time in my life in which I needed counseling. After several sessions, the counselor diagnosed me with a severe case of depression. Prior to the diagnosis, life just didn't have any meaning. Nothing mattered. Many days my will to die outweighed my desire to live. I was at a place that I lost sight of my dreams. I lost sight of who I was as a person. Surely, this trial would be the end of me. I thought I'd never make it through.

Depression can have you believing that all hope is gone and there is no way out of escaping the pain.

At this particular time in my life, everything I held on to seemed to crumble: marriage, relationships and ministry. I had endured incredible pain and oppression. I had lost much and at times, being happy seemed foreign to me.

Yes, God was there, but at times, He was so silent, and my soul was empty. You may ask how can a soul become empty? Very easily when the sorrows of life suck the life out of you.

God created us with a soul. And our soul is made up of three components: the mind, the will, and emotions.

When our minds are consumed with only the horrible experiences we are facing and when we don't replace those thoughts with the Word of God, it's quite easy to get pulled into meditating all day on those bad experiences.

The emotions comprise many things, including love, hatred, joy, and grief.

Sometimes the decisions we make come out of our emotions. And our emotions can misdirect us; they are not trustworthy. We can be very emotional creatures; and at times, those emotions can be uncontrollable. Where we are right now is due to the fact that a choice was made. Most of us have made very wise and some very foolish decisions in life. If you look over the course of your life, I'm sure you would have done some things differently.

Have you considered how your life would be different if you had married someone else; if you hadn't slept with that person; what it would have been like if you'd taken that other job; moved into a different neighborhood; how rich you would be if you'd won the lottery; or what if you hadn't gotten that divorce? Do you see how our emotions can get the best of us?

My counselor was a Christian, so she would remind me of certain scriptures that I knew. But because I had allowed my situation to become my focus, those same scriptures that I quoted before somehow got lost in all the sadness I was experiencing.

Depression is no joke. It wasn't until my counselor diagnosed me that I began to research the causes and symptoms of depression. For me it was one word. Trauma. I had experienced an extremely stressful time in which I felt helpless and emotionally out of control. Yes, the events at that time left me traumatized. I was stuck. I felt paralyzed.

How could I move past this? Would I allow these conditions to hold me back from achieving my goals or ideal vision of success for me? Did I even know what success looked like?

Our will is what gives us the ability to make choices. Here is where the power to move forward must prevail. Our will must be the driving force that channels our success. Without it, doom and failure will be lurking at the door.

But Paul tells us like this:

"Finally, brethren, whatsoever things are true, whatsoever things are honest, whatsoever things are just, whatsoever things are pure, whatsoever things are lovely, whatsoever things are of good report; if there be any virtue, and if there be any praise, think on these things."

Philippians 4:8 (KJV)

There is a reason why Paul wrote this passage of scripture. It is for people like me. It is for people like you. People who need to be reminded of the promises in the Bible. I couldn't change my past, but I could change how it affected me.

The power to choose was mine. Would I allow these moments to break me or would I allow these moments to push me out of my comfort zone to live a life on my own terms?

Was it too late for a new beginning? Was it too late for God to turn my mourning into dancing? God's answer was "No."

How could God turn my mess into a message, turn my pain into joy, and allow me to win in life when the score appeared to be a thousand to one? Even with tears in my eyes, I had to convince myself my life mattered and that God was bringing me to a better place. I'd be the first to admit I was too busy adding up my problems instead of counting my blessings. I drastically needed a mind shift.

This mind shift included not giving up on myself, my dreams or the goals that were tucked away in the back of my mind. I had to come to grips that it was okay for me to succeed in life, even when others tried to make me feel guilty about wanting more in life. I realized that some people are content right where they are, and those who want more deserve more, and those who aspire are criticized for not settling for mediocracy. I didn't need anyone's approval to succeed or anyone's permission to live my best life. I owed it to myself. After everything I had gone through— I. Deserved. It. It was one of the happiest moments in life when I got reintroduced to Paulette! Underneath all that pain was a woman full of strength, purpose, and determination. The strength to keep moving to be unstoppable, unbreakable, and walk in my own power.

I was reminded of a passage of scripture where Paul was counting up his adversities, yet this is the same Paul who wouldn't allow the adversities to get him to lose sight of his destiny and purpose for living.

"Five different times the Jews gave me their terrible thirty-nine lashes. Three times I was beaten with rods. Once I was stoned. Three times I was shipwrecked. Once I was in the open sea all night and the whole next day. I have traveled many weary miles and have been often in great danger from flooded rivers and from robbers and from my own people, the Jews, as well as from the hands of the Gentiles. I have faced grave dangers from mobs in the cities and from death in the deserts and in the stormy seas and from men who claim to be brothers in Christ but are not. I have lived with weariness and pain and sleepless nights. Often, I have been hungry and thirsty and have gone without food; often I have shivered with cold, without enough clothing to keep me warm."

2 Corinthians 11:24-28 (TLB)

Although I faced much adversity, I learned to pick myself back up. I found hope and courage to walk many nights alone knowing that God was my defense and my counselor. Every test I've withstood only brought me closer to God and the blessings He had for me.

How did I move from depression? It took much prayer, soul searching, and the ability to want to win. I had a mind shift because without it, I would not have made it.

That's what it takes: the mind to win and a mind to want better. I couldn't change the outcome of many of my situations, but I could shift my perspective on how I wanted the results to be different.

I learned that if I trusted in God and believed His promises, He would cause every situation and circumstance to work out for my good. My faith got me through my darkest hour, and my faith kept me going.

The journey hasn't been easy, but it has taught me to believe in myself even when others doubted me. To elevate higher, I must trust the process, no matter how hard, and believe with God all things are possible.

"But Jesus beheld them, and said unto them, With

men this is impossible; but with God all things are possible."

Matthew 19:26 (KJV)

I learned to dream big, believe far greater, knowing that I could do all things through Christ who gives me strength. I was created with a purpose and for a purpose. That purpose will continue to be fulfilled as I seek Him for guidance, leave myself open for change, and explore opportunities that are presented.

"I can do all things through Christ which strengthened me."

Philippians 4:13 (KJV)

I can look back over my life and see how God has blessed me tremendously. As an award-winning author, I have been featured in many periodicals, including the *Sacramento Observer;* Featured author on two magazine covers: and best inspirational romance winner for my book "Secret Places Revealed." My journey has taken me all over the world with countless online radio interviews sharing my story of hope as well as my experiences as an author.

I have a thriving business where I mentor and coach aspiring authors. My expertise in promoting books has opened up great doors of opportunities as I'm called upon to share my knowledge.

I pulled this from my book "Completely Whole," and I believe it's worth repeating. When I wrote this, I thought about how life comes to beat us up, break us down, and leave us scarred. But God has other plans for us.

> *"For I know the thoughts that I think toward you, saith the Lord, thoughts of peace, and not of evil, to give you an expected end."*
>
> *Jeremiah 29:11 (KJV)*

Still I Rise

I've been beaten, scorned and battered … Still I Rise.

I've been devalued … Still I Rise.

My spirit has been crushed… Still I Rise.

My heart is broken… Still I Rise.

Oppressed by people… Still I Rise.

Homeless … Still I Rise.

Faced death … Still I Rise.

Storm, rain, and floods… Still I Rise.

In debt, discouraged, and broke… Still I Rise.

Adversities come to wipe us out… Still I Rise.

Struggling with drugs and alcohol… Still I Rise.

Accusations and vocal assaults… Still I Rise.

The enemy has set traps to get me to fall… Still I Rise.

Mountains, hurdles, obstacles stand in my way… Still I Rise.

Miscarriage … Still I Rise.

Divorced and alone… Still I Rise.

Lost everything… Still I Rise.

Catastrophe, testing, and trials… Still I Rise.

Suffering because of my faith… Still I Rise.

Hated … Still I Rise.

Misunderstood… Still I Rise.

Lied upon… Still I Rise.

Molested … Still I Rise.

In distress and perils on every side… Still I Rise.

A woman who soars is a woman who refuses to allow life to dictate her outcome! On many occasions we need to be reminded of where we are and how we got there. It is not the end of the story.

Yes, without a doubt I took the necessary steps to get where I am. I quit listening to those who have no idea where I'm going or what God is doing in my life. I've chosen to soar and live a life without regrets.

About the Author

 CRED

PAULETTE HARPER is an award-winning best-selling author of both fiction and nonfiction books. She is a sought-after speaker, pastor, coach and marketing specialist. Her mission, as a speaker, is to help women find hope through transformation, restoration and reclaiming their lives through workshops, conferences and seminars. As a book coach, she helps authors and aspiring authors grow their book business by providing marketing strategies, tools, resources, and opportunities to help them succeed in the literary world.

Her literary works have been spotlighted in a growing number of publications, including CBN, Real Life Real Faith Magazine, The Sacramento Observer and Black Pearls Magazine. She has also appeared on numerous local and online radio shows. Paulette is also the owner of Write Now Literary Book Tours, an online service to help promote authors.

Paulette lives in Northern California.

To book Paulette for your next event contact her: paulette@pauletteharper.com

Visit her at: www.pauletteharper.com

SOARING INTO PURPOSE

ೞೞ

Rev. Dr. Elaine Gattis, DMin.

The Call

The LORD had said to Abram, "Go from your country, your people and your father's household to the land I will show you.

Genesis 12:1 (NIV)

The words that God spoke to Abram in Genesis 12:1 are the same as God spoke to me. Over twelve years ago, the call from God to "Go" was deeply engrained in my spirit when I left my family and home in the San Francisco Bay Area and relocated to Atlanta, Georgia. At the time, I knew very little about Atlanta. I had visited once to attend a ministry conference, but Atlanta was otherwise unfamiliar territory for me. Nevertheless, there was a burning burden in my spirit to get there.

Many people describe the call of God as something that you simply cannot ignore; this was true for me. I believed God had something more for me there. Something of purpose was waiting for me. Something that would make life more meaningful. I remember having a sense that if I did not make the move, a huge piece of my life's puzzle would be missing. Atlanta was essentially my Promised Land. For me, it was the place where my purpose in God would be realized.

A Quantum Leap of Faith

Some may give little thought to packing up and moving over two thousand miles from their birthplace. Yet, when you are a single parent who has never lived more than ten miles away from your family and support system, two thousand miles was a monumental undertaking for me—mentally and emotionally.

Oh, and did I mention I was leaving behind a sixteen-year-old daughter. My only child, Armoriana, wanted to remain to finish her last two years of high school. I was also leaving a home I owned in California, ownership of my hair salon and a catering business.

To be clear, I was going to Atlanta with approximately three months savings and no employment prospects. I would be moving into a one-bedroom apartment that I found on the Internet. I had completed my first year of graduate school in California and had received an offer for a full-time position at the same seminary. In actuality, the job offer was a dream come true, as I had long hoped to teach or become an administrator at a college or university.

Life was good for me in California. Yet, something was missing. I remember having a conversation with my mother and telling her I needed to spread my wings and fly. When considering all I was walking away from, it would seem that I had lost my mind. However, I had a Word from God to "Go"!

God had blessed me to be spiritually mature and grounded. Having spent years as a licensed minister and fully engulfed in the Word of God, my faith in God was on solid footing. I was a woman who was confidently depending on the direction and the leading of God. I had very profound dreams and encounters with the Holy Spirit, and I could see God moving in my life and could clearly hear God's voice. On separate occasions, two different people spoke prophetically to me that I would move to Atlanta, and I received prophetic revelation that God had much in store for me there. This further confirmed the Word the Lord had already given me. Therefore, I left California and everything I loved.

The Battle before the Promise

"Be strong and very courageous. Be careful to obey all of the law my servant Moses gave you; do not turn from it to the right or the left, that you may be successful wherever you go. Keep this Book of the Law

always on your lips; meditate on it day and night, so that you may be careful to do everything written in it. Then you will be prosperous and successful. Have I not commanded you? Be strong and courageous. Do not be afraid; do not be discouraged, for the Lord your God will be with you wherever you go."

Joshua 1:7-9 (NIV)

In the above passage, God was adamant about Joshua understanding the need to be strong and courageous. God promised to be with him as he led the children of Israel into the land that God had promised. What God already knew, and Joshua may not have quite understood, is that he was about to engage in some of the greatest warfare of his lifetime. Given what was ahead of him, he would need all the strength, all the courage, and all the faith that was within him. Above all, Joshua needed to know God would be with him wherever he went and during whatever he faced.

Upon the Lord's instruction, Joshua prepared the children of Israel to "take possession" of the Promised Land. He informed the tribes that they would cross the Jordan to the Promised Land. However, before any one of them would be able to occupy and rest in the land, their soldiers would first have to take possession of it (Joshua 1:12-15 NIV). Essentially, they were going to have to fight for their promise!

I left California on a red-eye March 3, 1996, the evening of my daughter's sixteenth birthday. As soon as my plane landed at the Hartsfield-Jackson Airport in Atlanta, at the feeling of the wheels hitting the landing strip, my stomach sank for the very first time. I thought about all that I had just left behind. Leaving my daughter, my family and friends, my businesses and my home hit me like a ton of bricks. I remember thinking *What did I just do?*

I had spent many of my teenage years battling depression. As a young adult, I was diagnosed with clinical depression after years of distress and anxiety. Additionally, I suffered from postpartum depression after my daughter's birth. My spiritual growth enabled me to overcome those years. Since I was now separated from my support base, I feared slipping back into that dark place.

Christian friends often express a desire to take possession of the "promises of God." While I believe that it is good and necessary to pursue your purpose and the promises of the Lord, I must caution toward the old adage, "be careful what you ask for." Like Joshua, the Word of God was on my side, and by faith, I was standing on God's Word. What I was not aware of was the level of emotional and spiritual warfare that I would soon face. I did not know how much strength, courage and faith I would need for the journey ahead.

I'd left California thinking foremost about reaching my Promised Land. I thought about the promise of success from the Lord, and I wanted to take ahold of everything the Lord had for me. I didn't know exactly what that was, but I knew deep in my heart it was more than I had and more than I was. First Corinthians 2:9 (NIV) declares that *"eye has not seen, nor ear heard, nor have entered into the heart of man the things which God has prepared for those who love Him."* Paul goes on to say in verse 10, "*But God has revealed them to us through His Spirit. For the Spirit searches all things, yes, the deep things of God.*" While I had no clue what I was searching for, my spirit was well aware there was so much more and something much deeper that God had in store for my life.

Yet, despite the hope of God's promise, my spirit had quickly become broken by isolation, fear, and uncertainty. Moreover, from the moment my plane hit the ground, it seemed as though I stopped hearing the voice of God; my dreams and my vision had become clouded by the reality of being alone. I could no longer see or hear God. I felt abandoned by God and in disbelief that God would leave me at such a pivotal and vulnerable time in my life. "Where are you, God?" was the question that haunted me for several months. But God is faithful, and in hindsight,

I found that God never left me.

Possessing the Promise

Before leaving California, I had applied to the Emory University Candler School of Theology. My hope and goal was to complete my degree at Candler. When I left California, I had not yet received an acceptance letter from Emory, which was the only school where I'd applied. I was originally thinking of applying to a different school, however, I met one of the Candler professors at a conference before leaving California. I mentioned I was thinking about moving to Atlanta and he encouraged me to apply to Candler. He went as far as putting me in touch with a contact in Emory's administration who helped me with the application process. I didn't know much about Emory at the time and didn't realize how much of a long shot it would be to get into such a prestigious university.

There I was in Atlanta. I didn't have a job, nor was I in school. I didn't have any friends or family, and I was living in a tiny apartment. I was not hearing from God and had no clue as to what would happen next. Yet, I never felt the urge to return home. Despite my fears and uncertainty, I continued to hold on to the Word that was planted deeply in my heart and spirit. I could not shake the belief that there was a reason I was supposed to be in Atlanta.

As God would have it, things began to shift. In mid-April, a month after my arrival, I received an acceptance letter to begin classes at Emory in the Fall. By the end of April, God had blessed me with a job. By October, God enabled me to purchase a townhome. And, during my first semester at Emory, on the first night of class, I met Terrance, a man who would change the trajectory of the rest of my life.

Emory is a vast campus, and at night some of the areas of the campus are dark and desolate. I would often park in the Peavine parking deck and Terrance would walk me to my car to ensure my safety. We would literally spend hours standing in the parking garage after class, talking about life and debating our theological views, often until after midnight. We became the best of friends. Two years later, in that same Peavine parking deck, my best friend asked if I would become his wife. Today, we have been together for over twelve years and happily married for over nine. We have since obtained doctorate degrees and are serving in ministry together at a growing and thriving church where Terrance is the Senior pastor and I am the Executive pastor. We are both professors at a local university, authors, and conference speakers. God is using us in ways we never imagined and we are living a blessed and full life!

Throughout this journey, I was constantly reminded of something that my daughter said when she was just a teen. I was new to preaching, and one day as I was preparing to preach, I was nervous and terrified about what I would say. She said, "Mom, you already know the Word. It's in you." Indeed, it was! During this journey of uncertainty, fear, isolation, and finally triumph, I remained confident about the Word that God had given me. I *knew* what God said, but I had to learn to *trust* God's guidance even when I couldn't trace God. I could not see it at the time, but God's presence was always evident in the fruit that was manifesting in my life, in the blessings, in the provision, and in the grace that God was providing. Through my journey, I learned that the Lord, my God, would be with me wherever I go. Now, I *know* and now, I soar!

ABOUT THE AUTHOR

છ૪૦

DR. ELAINE GATTIS is a native of the San Francisco Bay Area. She is an educator, author, speaker, and ordained minister of the Gospel who holds a bachelor's degree in business administration from California State University, East Bay, a master of divinity degree from the Emory University Candler School of Theology, and a doctor of ministry degree from the Morehouse School of Religion at the Interdenominational Theological Center in Atlanta. She is an Associate Professor at Ohio Christian University's Morrow, Georgia campus, and serves as the Executive Pastor of Mt. Olive Baptist Church in Stockbridge, Georgia, where her husband, the Reverend Dr. Terrance Gattis serves as the Senior Pastor. Together, they have four adult children, Terrell, Tiana, Armoriana, and Nandi.

For more information visit www.elainegattis.com.

UNSHAKABLE FAITH
"FROM SURVIVING TO THRIVING"

∞

Katrina Shaw

"My soul finds rest in God alone; my salvation comes from Him. He alone is my rock and my salvation; He is my fortress. I will never be shaken."

Psalm 62:1-2 (NIV)

As a survivor of breast cancer, I tell you, it is not easy. We must continue to trust God. Stay focused, stay healthy with premium nutrition, exercise and most importantly keep our stress level down. The type of breast cancer I was diagnosed with is known as Estrogen and Progesterone Positive, so I was told that I had to eat all natural and organic foods. I now have to eat foods with no hormones, steroids, artificial flavoring, etc. So, watching what I eat is a challenge in itself because I have to be very selective. I'm that woman you will see in the grocery store checking all the ingredients on the labels before I purchase them. That is why I made the decision to take and promote an all-natural health and wellness supplement, thanks to a dear friend of mine. It's a premium product that is designed to fill any nutritional gaps and has a ton of great benefits, maintaining my overall health, mentally and physically. In addition, it keeps my body at an alkaline state, which is much needed as a survivor. I always say, "I thank God first and my *Thrive* supplement second."

Keeping my stress levels down this past year has been a real challenge for me. We all handle loss, grief, and trials of life in different ways, but the true test of faith is how we respond to it when it comes. I will never forget the dreaded day my faith was tested. I received a phone call from my father right after Valentine's Day. He stated, "Katrina, your mother is leaving us. The doctors have her on oxygen, and her organs are starting to shut down." I replied, "Dad, tell her to hold on. I'm coming, but if she goes before I get there, please don't move her." I had been watching my mother die slowly throughout the years. That was so hard for me to hear.

Well, after hanging up with my dad, I lost it. I was at work. I told my managers and coworkers. A few of them took me in the conference room and prayed with me. My only concern was that I make the three-hour drive to see her before she passed. I prayed and asked God to please allow me to be with my mother as she transitioned. I poured out my heart. "God, I want to hold her hand, pray with her, sing to her, and tell her it's okay." God had already prepared me for that day.

You see, seventeen years ago, my mother had a stroke that should have taken her life, but she survived by the grace of God. She developed dementia from the stroke. I remember when the doctors told the family about her diagnosis; it was unbelievable. *NO, not my Mother!!* A mother who was so loving, vibrant, God-fearing, my rock, and my best friend. The only way I could handle it was to not think about the later moments when she may not remember me. I had to focus on the present and cherish those moments. I prayed and asked God to give me the strength. Seeing my mother in the last stages of her disease was devastating. She was bedridden, on a feeding tube, and could not talk. Her beautiful smile was all I had to look forward to when I would visit.

My husband is a tractor trailer driver and was off work the day I got the news, so he was able to drive me to see my mom. *Thank God!!* While on the road, halfway en route, my dad called and asked where we were. He was afraid I would not make it there in time. My mother's health was failing quickly. *But GOD!!!* We made it there in time. God had answered my prayer. I held my mother's hand, sang to her and prayed with her until she transitioned. She actually held on three more hours after we arrived.

Losing a parent is extremely difficult, especially not having her there with me while I was going through my cancer diagnosis and surgery. I was reminded of twenty years prior. We had a conversation in the basement of the house where I'd grown up. She was washing clothes. I blurted out, "Mom, I hope I die before you." She asked why. I then told her I didn't want to go through the pain. It was devastating when I lost my only sister. She died suddenly of a brain tumor rupture. Her death was so painful that I had suicidal thoughts. My sister was my idol; we were extremely close. I did not want to feel that type of pain again. My mother looked at me and said, "When the time comes, you will be okay."

Sitting there with her twenty years later, I realized she was right. I was okay. God had prepared us and made it bearable, seeing her in such a state. It's amazing when you put your faith and trust in God. He will give you the strength you never thought you had. Isaiah 40:29 (NIV) records, *"He gives strength to the weary and increases the power of the weak."* As a survivor, I am reminded often by my doctor to do whatever I can to keep my stress levels down. So, remaining grounded in the word of God and staying focused is what gives me peace.

Unexpected Interruptions

Four months after my mother's passing, I lost my job of fifteen years. I did not see that coming. Every year, around budget time, there were cuts across the region. For years, I observed others coming and going but never thought it would be me. A reduction was enforced, and I and a few others were in that number. I had a lot of mixed feelings: shock, anger, happiness, then sadness. God knew it was time for me to move on, especially with the death of my mother. I really needed some time. I was blessed to get a good severance package. Thank God, I was able to get under my husband's insurance quickly. When one has a health challenge, they can't be without insurance. This was a blessing to me. I needed the break, and my job was getting a bit stressful. I had never lost a job before. I had always worked. Therefore, I had a lot of mixed emotions. While we may not be able to undo what is done nor understand, we can learn from it. We must change our thoughts to positive ones, move on, have faith and trust that God will make a way. Proverbs 3:5-6 (NKJV) says, *"Trust in the Lord with all your heart and lean on your own understanding, in all your ways acknowledge him and he will direct your paths."*

Well, I now had all the time in the world and wanted to wait at least three months before job searching. I was thankful to be able to spend more time with my dad. Wouldn't you know, I also ended up attending a total of seven funerals of close family and friends last year. Before the last funeral, I was so done. I told myself, "I am not attending anymore funerals unless it's someone very close to me." Unfortunately, it was. Thank God for his grace and mercy.

Surprising Opportunities – Thriving

After enduring those trying times, God began to send unexpected blessings through various opportunities. My first opportunity came while I was out of work. I went to my annual breast doctor's appointment. Toward the end of the appointment, she complimented me on how well I was doing. I told her I was doing well, feeling great and using *Premium Nutrition*. I was grateful for the doctors. I was blessed having my diagnosis caught early and was able to share my breast cancer story. She told me the hospital's marketing department was doing a social media campaign and got me in touch with the contact person before I left her office that day. The marketing person asked me to tell my story in more detail. After hearing my testimony, he said, "I'm going to talk to my editor because we'd rather use your story for our magazine, social media, and website. You can really help a lot of women." He told me to look out for an email from him in a few weeks. Sure enough, I heard from him. He set up an interview to cover the story followed by a photo shoot with the location of my choice. I was so excited to be in *Johns Hopkins Magazine,* on their website, and social media pages. The magazine came out in February 2018.

My next opportunity came while I was still out of work. It was my first book collaboration, *Unstoppable Warrior Women.* Out of twenty-five other women, I was one chosen to share my story. My photo shoot for Johns Hopkins, and the photo shoot for the book headshots were in the same week. God is so amazing. I have been thriving in opportunities that only God knew were coming!

Recently, as it began to draw closer to the end of the year, I started to worry; I was on pins and needles because I was still out of work. My father, hubby, and brothers were also getting a bit concerned. My severance was due to end at the beginning of the new year. So, I began searching the Internet for jobs in my profession. My friend told me to check out a particular place of employment, which she had mentioned to me several times. Yet, I never moved on it. Well, one day I finally applied. Then I went in to take a shower. By the time I came out, my cell phone was ringing. It was the company my friend referred. I had an interview that same week and got hired. *BUT GOD…* Back in my field of work with a great company. Let me tell you how God worked this thing out. My severance pay ended a week before my first check at my new job. *PRAISE BE TO GOD*!!

Through all the difficult challenges I had to face, I stood unshakable in faith and continued to trust God. He always has a plan for our purpose in life. He uses our story for His glory!

I have learned through overcoming challenges in life that we have to train ourselves to find the blessing in every situation. When I realized God put me through these challenges to be a witness for Him and glorify His name, there was no way that I would not share my story. Whenever there is an opportunity for me to share my story, I am grateful. There are too many women getting diagnosed with breast cancer every year, and too many who just get regular mammogram screening. That is the reason I started a blog on Facebook called *M.A.N.E.* which stands for "Mammograms are not Enough" to educate women of the importance of not only getting regular mammograms, but the knowledge that they are not enough. We as women need to demand what we want and be proactive. We have one life and one body.

"Do you not know that your bodies are temples of the Holy Spirit, who is in you, whom, you have received

from God. You are not your own."

First Corinthians 6:19 (NIV)

It's blessed to be a blessing. My purpose in life is to use my gifted talent to be a blessing and an inspiration to others by letting God use me. God enables me to stand for Him. I want to be the kind of woman that someone will look at and say, "Because of you, I didn't give up." I want my life to display the beauty of God.

"She has done a beautiful thing to me."

Mark 14:6 (NIV)

About the Author

⚜

KATRINA SHAW was born and raised in Long Island, New York and is a Morgan State University graduate. A radio and media professional of over twenty years, she currently works for Hearst Television, Inc. She is also a member of Delta Sigma Theta Sorority, Inc.

An entrepreneur, Katrina is pursuing her dream and passion to promote health and wellness with a product called "Thrive" by Le-vel and is making an impact to change lives and help others.

A five-year breast cancer survivor, she created a Facebook blog page, MANE (Mammograms are Not Enough), and supports and enlightens women on the importance of diagnostic mammogram/3D screenings. She desires to give support to other survivors, those going through the process of a diagnosis, or who have loved ones affected by the disease.

At the end of 2018, MANE will be launched as a business assisting with funding for women without insurance or adequate coverage for extra screenings and other medical fees and expenses associated with the disease.

Katrina resides in Baltimore, Maryland with her husband. She is very involved in her community and church. A Zumba Fitness Instructor, she enjoys traveling, reading, and serving as a role model to at-risk youths.

Contact Katrina at her website: www.thrivin4better.com.

MY LIFE REBOOT

❧

Roni J. Teson

Fourteen-hour workdays were my norm. For years, I had this crazy-intense focus on getting the job done by way of exceeding all expectations.

That clock stopped when I lost my hair.

After that, no matter how hard I tried, I never found my way back to my old life.

***

My doctor decided to be aggressive with my treatment. I allowed that course of action. What did I have to lose? Breast cancer had already seeped into my bones.

"What's my prognosis?"

"Don't know," my doctor said. "We have to see how you respond to the medicine." My mind drifted as she spoke in *multi-syllabled chemotherapy words* that probably described my future.

"Any questions?" she asked.

Tons. But I don't know where to start.

When she escorted me toward the appointment

window, a woman in scrubs passed by wearing a knowing smile. Our eyes connected, but she looked away. Shuffling behind her, a frail woman with a scarf over her bald head and a man carrying her purse, gripping her elbow.

I froze.

Did I just witness my future? I might as well have pulled the trigger myself. For three months, I walked around with a lump in my breast and did nothing about it.

Now, I'm a dead girl walking.

How many months, weeks, days did I have left in this skin? My muscles tightened like tentacles wrapping around my neck and traveling down my spine. Why did I always have to excel in everything? Why couldn't I have started at stage one or two . . . or even three?

In my hard-earned executive position at work, I never took time off. For the previous two years I rolled up my sleeves, travelled weekly, and did whatever needed to be done to save my employer from bankruptcy. We had finally begun operating out of the red about the time chemo kicked my butt.

Through the first two rounds of treatment, I worked from home. I rocked the phones and accomplished a lot. If I couldn't lift my head, I used a personal day. I'd banked enough hours to continue on that path for a while. But my employer had different plans.

"I can work part-time. I can be whole, financially," I said to my boss, Dave, on our weekly call. I'd read the company's disability policy. Our insurance paid sixty percent of my income and I could earn the other forty percent working part-time.

He sighed, loud enough for me to hear it through the phone.

"What's wrong?" I leaned back in my chair and stared at the many piles of papers that had accumulated in my home office. Multiple heights on every available surface: the makings of marketing and operational strategies—the positions I'd covered for two years. Old school printed paper, wasted trees.

Wasted time.

"I know half of you is better than a hundred percent of most people." A distinct sucking noise came through the phone. Dave only smoked in times of extreme stress. "This is the hardest conversation I've ever had. I'm going to represent the corporation first, then I'm speaking to you as a friend."

He took another puff.

"You're smoking again?"

Like the swinging of a hammer, he exhaled and said, "We feel you should just take time off and get well."

"But I'm—"

"It's not a choice."

"Oh."

I had never *not* had a job. What would I do with myself on my good days? Sulk in cancer dread?

"As a friend," he said. "I can't stay here another minute. I'm quitting."

Wait a minute. No!

Dave contacted me when he became president. He recruited me. We'd been through so much together. We saved the company from financial ruin. I couldn't be hearing him right.

"So, you're leaving?"

"Yes, I'm done."

He never shared details of what made him angry enough to join the unemployed so abruptly, but it seemed as if his fast exit had something to do with my situation.

I would have followed Dave to the moon, but I couldn't make a job move then—no hair, no travel, and I didn't even know if I'd survive. For the first time ever, I truly needed medical insurance.

I stayed.

Forced into disability, I felt as though I'd been dumped. I definitely didn't feel supported. But in my secret relief, I found a new distraction. I went back to work on the partially written novel that had grown cold during my workaholic phase.

My new focus became daily email exchanges with a writing coach I knew well from years before. That set my sail soaring. Through six rounds of harsh chemo, surgery, and radiation (nine-plus months of torture), I wrote and rewrote my novel.

An amazing thing occurred with this beautiful new distraction. Just as I finished the final draft of my novel, my cancer went into remission. I'd sent my characters into Hell (literally) and brought them through the final scene changed (with a Hollywood ending). My optimistic written words had somehow elevated my fate.

Stage IV cancer in remission, a miracle worthy of celebration. But that didn't happen. More trials lay ahead.

Fuzzy mind, fuzzy hair, fuzzy life . . .

***

Weeks later, from my new-to-me rental house by the beach, I still tried to ignore the most painful part of the last eleven months. It wasn't the cancer.

After eight-plus years of togetherness, my love ran away with another woman. I survived cancer, but my relationship did not.

I sat on my leather sofa, staring at the peek-a-boo view of the ocean and the smudged outline of Catalina Island twenty-seven miles away. Boxes stuffed full of things from *our* house still lined the edges of the living room.

My life reboot had been launched: a new employer, a rental at the beach. A solo life. My finances were rickety at best after cancer. But I found a way to move near the ocean, and I would find a way to stay.

I hoped.

And then I got the call from my doctor's office. "It's a good news/bad news situation," she said. "Which do you want first?"

"Shoot straight the way you always do."

"One of the biopsies is malignant."

Again?

I bicycled twice a day. I worked out. I ate healthy. How could this be?

I pulled the hoodie over my short hairs and headed outside. I didn't remember my doctor sharing any *good news* or how I ended the call, but I was no longer in a conversation. I thought I'd walk along the beach. My feet chose a different path. I cut across Pacific Coast Highway and rounded the corner. I walked faster when I saw the blue exterior of my dad's house. He'd left his garage door open. I tapped on the interior door and poked my head inside.

"Are you home?"

Dad sat at the kitchen table with a stack of paperwork in front of him. He'd retired, but he always had something going on. I walked past him to the slider, glanced at a stalk of corn growing from a planter on his deck adjacent to the harbor.

"I don't know what to do," I said. "More cancer. Totally unrelated to the first one." *Oh God, I'm still in treatment for the first one.* "What am I gonna do?"

Dad dropped his eyeglasses on the papers. "You're gonna get it cut out. Then you're gonna get up and get moving."

"What if I get more cancer? What if it comes back?"

"You keep getting it cut out. You keep getting up. That's all there is to it."

I gripped the doorframe with my fingertips and pressed my nose against the glass. An overwhelming sense of separation from the world swept through me.

"We'll deal with it," Dad said as if he could read my mind.

My shoulders were practically pinned to my ears when I thought about the complete unraveling of my life. Yet every day, since I'd moved to the beach alone, I'd picked up my guitar and strummed a tune, belted out a song. After a few times of singing louder and louder, I fully comprehended my liberation. I often woke up early and went straight to work on my laptop, *clickity-clack* free to tap. No heavy huffing or whining from anybody.

My writing. My music. My life.

I relaxed my shoulders. *I can do this.*

Dad gestured toward the stalk of corn. "You like that?"

I took a deep breath, pushed away thoughts of another cancer growing in my body, another woman living my life. "I think it's really cool, Dad. Who grows corn in the harbor? It's amazing."

"It's self-sustaining. I'll show you."

He slid the door open, and I followed him onto the deck. I'd never seen a stalk of corn growing by itself. It stood as tall as me. He showed me how he loaded the water every three weeks.

I touched a leaf. "It's sturdy."

"It's trick."

Trick, my dad's favorite word since 1972, made me smile.

"I want a planter like this." I wanted a stalk of corn for myself. No more restrictions in my life, ever again.

"I'll give you the information about where I bought it," Dad said.

"Maybe I can grow tomatoes on my deck?"

"I'll bet you can."

I left Dad with his stack of papers. He'd given me honest-to-goodness relief, helped me right my course. I felt much better, which totally helped me deal with the fact that I wouldn't do the one thing I wanted to do the most—call my ex. I walked back home, climbed the stairs to my place, sat on the leather couch, and forced my fingers to dial my doctor's number instead.

"I'm sorry," I said. "I wasn't all there earlier. What happens next?"

"It's gotta come out."

"Surgery?"

She laughed. "Yeah, there's no other way to remove a thyroid."

I let out a long stream of air. *Another surgery. Damn.* I had survived forty-six years with no surgeries, no hospital stays, and no health issues until this mess.

***

Within days, I met my throat surgeon.

"You might end up sounding like this." He used a whispery voice. "Sometimes cancer is near the vocal cords. They get clipped and—

"No."

He stepped back as if I had offended him.

"I'm telling you, no. If cancer is near my vocal cords, sew me up. I'll find another way." I'd already lost my love, my house, my career, my finances, my dog . . . my hair. "You can't have my voice."

He blinked a few times. "But your life—"

"I mean it. Don't touch my vocal cords."

Later, when I woke up from surgery with a bandage on my throat and fog in my head, the surgeon greeted me with a smile and a celebratory nod. A moment I won't ever forget.

"Thank you." My voice worked! Hallelujah.

My situation really began to sink in—two cancers, a career collapse, and a broken heart—all within a twelve-month period. What other evidence did I need? My old life was gone forever.

Dammit me. I would not go down in a puddle of tears.

I would not waste another ounce of energy on the past.

I decided an incredible life was waiting for me—I just needed to head in that direction. And, that I did.

About the Author

❧

Roni Teson is a two-time Readers' Favorite award-winning novelist and the recipient of the First Place Dante Rosetti Award for YA Suspense Romance. Convinced that her passion for writing played a critical role in saving her life, Roni's entire perspective shifted when she beat stage IV cancer. Her soul-searching quest to understand the meaning of life's not so random coincidences has led her down a path of self-discovery and into an extraordinary existence. Read about her amazing life reboot in her most recent creation, *The Order of Things*.

Visit her at https://roniteson.com.

TEARS FOR MY SISTER

❧

Marcy Thomas

Some say, "there is no best friend like your sister." My sister Christine was that to me. Born two years apart with me being the oldest, she was very vocal and sassy. Christine knew how to get right close and personal with you if you made her angry. Her mouth got her into plenty of trouble as a child. Me, I was the laid back one. I avoided conflict like the plague. However, one thing for sure, Christine had my back when trouble would arise. I truly admired her boldness and tenacity. I always felt safe with her around.

We grew up in a two-parent home. My father, Dwight, was the strict disciplinarian and our Mother, Julia, was the encourager. She allowed us to participate in all kinds of activities like drill team, acting classes, singing in the choir, Girls Scouts, you name it. Our favorite pastime as a family was singing along with all the R& B artists. Dad and Mom both had awesome singing voices. They would teach us how to harmonize and keep our pitch while singing. Those times were my fondest memories of my childhood.

When I was about eleven years old, my parents announced my mother was pregnant. Our baby sister, Julia, was born on my mother's birthday. Then three years later our mother delivered our brother, Dwight Jr., who was born on Christine's birthday. Just as Christine predicted. My sister Christine and I were responsible for watching our younger siblings so that my mother could work and finish nursing school.

Christine and I began dating in our late teen years. I began seeing a guy named Paul, who was a few years older than myself. This relationship was short-lived due to an incident at a dance hall where I witnessed him dancing inappropriately with another young lady. When I voiced my displeasure to him, he became enraged, slapping me across my face so hard I saw stars. All I know is that everything faded to black! When my vision came into focus, Paul was on the ground holding his face. Apparently, I had punched him! Christine was rocking back and forth getting ready to pounce on him to finish the job. I quickly grabbed her, and we walked out of the building. When we got outside, I got an epiphany. This was not what I wanted for myself. Paul was controlling; he found fault in everything I said or did. I deserved to be treated with respect. *Georgia Coalition Against Domestic Violence states that one in three women and one in four men will experience physical violence by an intimate partner in their lifetime.*

In July 1982, I met my future husband, Alvin. He was kind, polite and very respectful to me. It took some time for me to totally trust him because of my past relationship. God truly answered my prayer. He was a man that loved and served God.

In August 1982, Christine met her future husband, J.H, at a wedding rehearsal. Christine had a beautiful singing voice, and J.H. also sang and played piano. They sang a rendition of Stevie Wonder's "A Ribbon in the Sky." The way they performed the song together showed there was an attraction between them. Their relationship grew quickly. When J.H was around our family and friends, he was outgoing and charismatic. Christine was still quick-tempered and didn't mind laying him out for standing her up for a date. I didn't like seeing my sister being taken for granted. He would always buy her something or find a way to get back in her good graces.

In January 1985, I had my first child and married Alvin in August 1985. Christine eloped with J.H. in October 1985. We did not hear from her for a month. I was disappointed because we told each other everything; our relationship was definitely changing. My parents were deeply troubled, as she was just eighteen years old. Finally, one day she called me, and

I convinced her and J.H. to come by my parents' house to talk. They came by. Everyone expressed their feelings about the elopement, and we moved on.

Christine surprised us one day with news that she was having a baby. We were very happy, yet, very much concerned after recognizing signs of J.H.'s control issues. The first incident I can remember was when Christine decided to cut her hair. We thought she looked beautiful, however J.H. was so negative and disrespectful. He said, "I didn't give you permission to cut your hair!" My parents looked at him like he was crazy. My sister said nothing. Later that day, my mother and I pulled her aside to ask if everything was alright. Christine had little to say about the incident. I could tell something was broken in her. Christine no longer had a voice in her marriage.

Christine delivered her first son, Isaiah, and two years later her second son, Michael, was born. Christine would confide in me that J.H. would ridicule her about her weight gain after her pregnancies. Then he began trying to isolate her from family and friends. All the signs were evident that she was in an abusive relationship. I wondered what happened to the sister I'd known growing up. Christine and J.H. separated several times throughout the marriage. She would either leave and go back or let him back into their home.

In April 2004, during a separation, J.H. became upset because Christine began setting boundaries. This did not go over well with J.H. He began to try to manipulate their sons with false accusations about Christine. Finally, she got to her "enough." Christine conveyed her true feelings and wanted to file for a divorce. The very next day, I received a call from Christine to meet her at the hospital. When I arrived, she was sitting in the waiting room visibly upset. I asked what happened. Christine began to tell me that the night before J.H. held her and the boys hostage by gunpoint all night. I felt the blood drain from my face. *God, no!* Christine said, "He must have realized how much it traumatized them. He got up the next morning and drove to another town to attempt suicide." My mother walked in and I began filling her in on what happened. We asked, "Where are the boys?" She said, "They are in school." Immediately, I thought about the boys possibly reporting what happened the night before to school officials. I told Christine, "You have to report this to the police." Christine was against the idea, admitting she was afraid that J.H. would retaliate in some way.

J.H. did survive the suicide attempt and was transferred to a mental facility. Christine finally agreed to report the incident and file for a Temporary Protection from Abuse Order. Afterwards, she made the decision to move herself and her sons in with my parents. J.H. continued to try to contact her through phone and emails. She would only communicate with him about their sons. J.H. knew there was no coming back from this. The marriage was over!

Christine continued to work and began planning for her future. She enrolled in community college for that Fall. An apartment she applied for was approved. She was feeling more and more confident, even though the harassment continued. She was determined to make a better life for her and her sons.

On June 17, 2007, Father's Day, my parents, brother, sister, sister-in-law, nephews, and children all gathered at my house for a barbecue. When Christine arrived with my nephews, I hugged her as she walked into my kitchen. She looked happier than I had seen her in a while. We all sang songs and told family stories that had us laughing and in tears. Every once in a while, I noticed Christine was glancing at her cell phone with a concerned look on her face. I asked if everything was okay. She told me J.H. was sending her messages that he wanted to see the boys. According to her, they did not want to see him, as the relationship was strained because of the previous incident.

After a few hours, Christine and the boys began preparing to leave to go home. I remember watching them get into her car. She did a U-turn on my street. I saw her say something to the boys, and they all laughed. They disappeared down the street, smiling and laughing.

The very next morning I was preparing to start my work day. The phone rang and I answered it to hear my mother sounding very urgent and nervous. She told me that something was going on. The boys had a very disturbing message from their father that he'd hurt their mother. My mother had been trying to call Christine's cell phone and job with no answer. I said, "I am on my way there to see what is going on."

I got off the phone and felt sick to my stomach. My husband and I were about twenty minutes away from Christine's job. We drove in an eerie silence that was unbearable. All I can remember saying to myself was the first line of Psalm 23 "*The Lord is my Shepherd.*" My nerves would not allow me to recall the remaining portion of the verse. *God, please don't let this be true. Please!!* When we pulled up into her workplace's parking, nothing looked out of order at first. Until we saw my sister-in-law running towards the back of the building. My husband and I jumped out the car following her, as the medical examiner arrived on the scene. My knees tried to buckle. We picked up our speed. When we turned the corner, we spotted her car in the middle of the parking lot with the driver's door open. The policemen at the scene tried to stop us. At that moment, my mother and my nephews drove into the parking lot. A policeman began asking us questions about who we were. We identified ourselves. Then he spoke those dreadful words: "I am sorry for your loss." Loss??? I was confused. He then said, "Your family member was parking her car when a suspect in another vehicle rammed his vehicle into hers, trapping her. He then shot her, killing her."

"No! No! No…" My husband took off running towards Christine's car. I saw police officers trying to hold him back from getting to the car. My mother wailed, and my nephews were in shock!! I looked towards the car where my sister's lifeless body remained.

This was surreal. *Think! Think…* I turned to a police officer. I said, "Sir, I believe her estranged husband is responsible. She had a protection order against him, and he has been harassing her. Check her work emails and her cell phone." My husband, mother and I gave him more information to help in their investigation.

After what seemed like an eternity, my mother and I drove to my parents' house to break the news to my father who was home nursing a leg injury. My sister-in-law took the boys with her to try to calm them down. I will never forget my mother sobbing uncontrollably, asking God to take this cup from her. I said nothing. I was numb! If I had known yesterday would be the last time I would hug her, I would have held her longer. Tighter. My sister—my very best and first friend—was gone! My heart and head began pounding again as we got off the exit to my parents' home. I remember watching people wash their cars and kids jumping rope. I felt an anger rise up within me. My thought was, *why are they acting like something terrible just didn't happen? We will never be the same again! God help me to understand why this happened!*

As we entered the house, my father was on the phone, still trying to get information about Christine. I looked into my father's eyes. He knew it wasn't good news. My mother began to tell him that Christine…was gone. My father broke down, and my mother began screaming. I stood in the middle of the living room feeling lost and the tears just flowed. *The Tears for My Sister, Christine.* They kept flowing and flowing. What fear she must have felt for her life. "God, we need you now," I said, sobbing.

Later that afternoon we were informed that J.H. was surrounded by police in the next town. He committed suicide in his vehicle. We couldn't imagine how the boys were feeling. Losing both parents in the same day. In such a tragic way. Our hearts ached for the boys. They loved their father. But their mom was their heart—and they were hers. The Bible says in *Lamentations 3:21-24 (ESV), "But this I call to mind, and therefore I have hope: The steadfast love of the Lord never ceases; his mercies never come to an end; they are new every morning; great is your faithfulness. 'The Lord is my portion,' says my soul, 'therefore I will hope in him.'"* When we put our trust in God, He is right there with us even during our darkest times.

Christine's funeral was a week later. She wore a tiara and a beautiful blush-pink colored dress. She was at rest now. No more pain. No more crying. And no more abuse. The most touching scene I witnessed during her service is when Christine's oldest son, Isaiah, took the handkerchief from the funeral director and gently draped it across her face. Her youngest son, Michael, helped tuck the blanket around her body as they closed her casket for the very last time. I saw young teen boys turning into young men right before my eyes. My tears flowed for my nephews as they were now motherless and fatherless.

What will our lives be like without her? Christine meant so much to so many people, which was evident in the many people that attended her service.

My family decided that the boys would live with my husband, three daughters and me. They have been the strongest young men I know, never missing an opportunity to share their story with their classmates and teachers. The support from our church, community and school district was amazing and instrumental in helping the boys to graduate on time. They are both adults now. I am sure it still hurts them to think about their parents and how their lives ended. I am sure they share *"Tears for My Sister."*

In Memory of Christine C. 1966-2007

In honor of my sister Christine, I have dedicated my life to educate, encourage and pray for all who have experienced Domestic Violence. Currently, I serve as a mentor for young women in groups and individually to help build self-esteem and self-worth in churches and community settings. I have had the opportunity to stand alongside community leaders and government officials as we advocate for Marsy' Law Bill of Equal Rights for Crime Victims in the state of Georgia. Each year I help facilitate informational sessions on Domestic Violence Awareness and Women's Health in my local church.

References: Georgia Coalition Against Violence

My hope is that my contribution to Women Who Soar helps teens and women discover that they deserve to be treated with respect, love, and to bring healing and hope into their lives. This epidemic crosses every economic, race, religion, age, and gender.

If you or anyone you know is in an abusive relationship,

please contact: The National Domestic Violence Hotline at 1-800-799-7233 (SAFE).

ABOUT THE AUTHOR

⊂⊃

MARCY THOMAS is an avid reader and book reviewer of Christian fiction. She has worked professionally as a certified medical coder for eighteen years. In 2008, Marcy was certified as a domestic violence advocate through The Domestic Abuse Project in Delaware County, Pennsylvania after the murder of her sister Christine. As an advocate, she's had opportunities to speak about domestic violence at churches, health fairs, schools, and youth groups.

In 2011, she was appointed Vice-President of The Project Butterfly in Chester, PA for two years. The Project Butterfly was an organization geared toward teaching teen girls to understand the difference between healthy and unhealthy relationships. Marcy's passion helping teen girls and women understand they should have self-love first and realize they are fearfully and wonderfully made.

Marcy resides in Covington, Ga with her husband, Alvin, of thirty-three years. She has three adult daughters, two nephews she raised and two gifted grandchildren.

You can contact her for speaking engagements at: marcythomas.selflove@gmail.com.

FLYING ABOVE THE STORM

❦

Shurvone Wright

My Beginnings

Growing up, I somehow knew I would overcome my circumstances. I knew my life had more meaning, and I would make a mark in the world in some way. This is my journey and how I overcame, how I learned to fly above the storm.

I am a woman that loves to help and motivate others. I believe I was placed on this planet to inspire others to grow and change.

I was born and raised in the San Francisco Bay Area. I had a very difficult childhood with many challenges, heartaches and experiences a young person should not have to see nor live through. I always had an inner strength and a knowing that I would be okay. Now, I understand it was the Holy Spirit; I had a fight inside of me that allowed me to always fight for my peace and a better life.

I moved multiple times in my youth because my grandparents cared for me about ninety percent of the time. Then, my grandfather died when I was nine, and

I remember thinking my life would never be the same. From that day forward, I felt alone and unprotected.

My parents would pick me up when it was convenient or when they would get it together enough to have me for a short time. I was shifted back and forth until I was 18 years old, when I decided to move out of the house.

During that time, I was lost and did things I am ashamed of today. I was a shy and insecure young woman. I knew I had purpose; I just did not know what or where to start. When I was 21 years old, another life defining age, I was faced with a decision to live or die. I was doing things and living a fast lifestyle that would have led to my demise if I did not get out. I remember lying in bed, depressed, not knowing what to do or to whom to turn. Then, as clear as day, I heard a voice say, "You are going to die if you don't stop now" That day my life changed forever, and I began the journey toward a nursing career of 31 years.

I went on to nursing school. It took me two years to complete my program. After graduating from nursing school, I married my first husband who was abusive and very controlling. The marriage lasted three years until I walked out one day after he left for work. At the time, I was working at a substance-abuse clinic in San Francisco, California. I left with one paycheck and the clothes I owned.

A few years later, at age twenty-two, I was blessed with my first nursing position. I was working in patient contact care on a medical surgical floor in Pasadena, California. I just knew I would practice as a nurse until I retired. I quickly learned how much I loved caring for people, helping and educating them on their care. Working in the nursing profession gave me many opportunities to do what I loved.

After that, I gained even more experience. I worked in hospitals, clinics, home care and drug and alcohol settings.

A few years later, I met and then later married my current husband of 25 years. I was twenty-eight by that time. Over the years, we have faced many obstacles, challenges and great times. Raising four daughters, I feel, gave us the greatest joy, also the greatest challenges. We have learned to lean on our faith to get us through.

Even today, I continue to lean on my faith for total guidance and direction. I have also learned how to have the courage to move forward in the face of fear, continuing to develop that inner strength that helps me to stand on the plan God has for me. Understanding that God will never give up on me and his promises will never fail have been my greatest lessons thus far.

"But those who hope in the Lord will renew their strength. They will soar on wings like eagles; they will run and not grow weary, they will walk and not be faint"

Isaiah 40:31 NIV

A Curve Ball

I finally landed a position in an office setting at Hill Physicians Medical Group. I enjoyed working behind the scenes, reviewing and authorizing services for patients. It was comfortable. I had amazing co-workers I called friends and life was indeed good. I was getting a great paycheck, but I still had some inner struggles. It was at this job that God started to prepare me for where I am today.

I requested counseling to assist in my growth process. One day, during a worksite counseling session, I asked for help with getting over being afraid to speak up in meetings and being bold enough to stand my ground in a professional manner. The counselor asked me how I thought others saw me. I rattled off all these amazing, positive things, which she wrote on a white board. Then she asked me how I saw myself. To my surprise, the list was very different. She then said, "You must learn how to be confident without regret." That was another life changing moment. The light bulb came on; I became very emotional because it was as if I finally had permission to own who I was and not be afraid of others' opinions. It was OKAY to love myself right where I was and along the way to where I was going. That day was the day my movement was born. I knew that God was going to do something with it I just did not know what at the time. So, I returned to my desk and quickly wrote *"Confidence Without Regret"* down and decided I was going to trademark the name, which I did. It took a year, but I did it. *So, when God gives you something, don't sit on it, move, and he will guide you every step of the way.*

Shortly after that experience, the homey type of environment of the workplace started to feel very corporate and less desirable. Then layoffs started happening, and I decided I was not going to wait around for them to lay me off. I started looking for a new job and found one. Things started off well, and I thought, "Okay, I can do this." Then things rapidly changed when I got a new boss. My work environment became very toxic to the point my doctor put me on medical leave.

Once that happened, I knew I was at a crossroad again in my life where I needed to make a very difficult decision. When faced with a very challenging decision in my life, I learned to pray, listen and wait on God. *What do you have in place when you are faced with difficult decisions? Do you get scared? Do you freeze up and don't do anything? Do you just wait and hope all things are going to work-out?*

During my prayer time at home, I remember thinking, "Lord, what am I going to do? I cannot go back to that toxic work place." Again, in the moments I needed clarity, I heard in my spirit, Call John, a financial professional. I could not believe what I was feeling. I had never talked to him about that career, and he never approached me in the three years we worked together in the community with the Chamber of Commerce. I was shocked, but I listened because I knew such a drastic change from nursing to an insurance agent could not have been coming from my own thoughts. Plus, I had now reached 52 years of age and would be starting a new career after thirty-one years in nursing. I was starting in something I knew nothing about, but I knew I could never give up on myself; I was ambitious.

Therefore, I called John and set an appointment, which turned into three appointments with me and two with my husband to make sure I was doing the right thing. After beginning the process of onboarding and studying for my licensing exam, I realized how much I loved what I was learning about the insurance industry and how I could use the information to help people. Suddenly, it dawned on me, "I am helping people treat their financial situations instead of their health situations." There I was again helping educate others. *When you are in the midst of making a big change, pay attention to how it fits the core of why God placed you here and that will certainly help you decide if you are going down the right path.*

So, I finished all the requirements for on boarding. I was ready to schedule and take the exam to become a licensed life insurance agent. I started to get nervous and make excuses in my head, "I can't do this. I am going to fail the test; I am not a good test taker." Needless to say, I canceled my exam the day before, crying to the person who helped with the onboarding process.

Have you ever talked yourself out of something new and exciting? Have you gotten so afraid of change you decided against it and wanted to remain comfortable?

That is what I almost did, stay comfortable and miserable in the job that I had come to hate. However, the counsel I received was to step back, believe in myself, go for it and to not **GIVE UP!** If I did, I would never know the outcome and never know what I could have accomplished. So, I rescheduled my exam and passed on the first try. I was so excited to know that God confirmed what I was supposed to do. Even with the little fear that had set in, I knew I had made the right decision.

Soaring

Once I started on my new journey and I had to start going to meetings, a little fear crept in again, and I told myself, "NEVER GIVE UP and turn off the FEAR in your mind." I was so intimidated by the entire process; I decided I had to do better, be better and perform better in all areas. I did not know how I was going to do it, but I knew I had to. I knew I had to develop a stance for NEVER GIVING UP! It was not easy; it was a daily process of conquering my fears. I learned how to meditate in the morning and at night. I had to pray and work at remembering all the things I am grateful for. I decided to not let fear control me. My new career had to work; there was no other option for me.

When you take that stance in your life, you start to see issues as opportunities to grow. You see more options and ideas to make things work. I also decided that whenever faced with bad days, I would NEVER GIVE UP ON ANYTHING. I would pray and meditate and believe that things would be better, and they did get better. *You must develop a belief in yourself. It must be stronger than your fears. You must make the decision, "No matter what, I am going to make it." When you do, watch what happens. Surround yourself with positive people and those that will encourage you and guide you.*

In my first year as an agent, I achieved a certain sales goals and was invited to attend an annual meeting honoring professionals who achieved this goal. I also earned multiple awards in my first year.

I monitor my feelings and make a conscious effort to switch off the nerves, intimidation and any overwhelming thoughts. It's an ongoing process, and I have worked hard to become the woman I am now. *You must also work hard, go after your dreams and always know that you have something to offer the world.*

In light of all I have experienced, I was led to start a closed Facebook group called *"Women's Empowerment Ministry: Confidence Without Regret."* There are over 340 women in the group. I had my first Women's Conference in 2017 with over 80 women in attendance. They all wore the T-shirt I designed, *"Confidence Without Regret."* This group helps to encourage women to live their best life and to be encouraged to love themselves along the way.

This journey has taught me to believe in myself, dream big and always remember I am capable of accomplishing anything I set out to do. I have learned how to control how long I allow any given situation to affect me and how to move on and conquer my fear whenever it tries to rear its ugly head. Nothing is impossible. So many amazing things has happened and more to come.

My business is thriving. I am now an author. I am traveling. I was featured in a company publication directed towards women due to my production and networking skills. I will soon travel to another one of their offices to train other agents. All because I decided to not let my fears hold me back and fly above the storm.

I must admit; on a daily basis, I have to work hard to stay above the storm. I listen to motivational videos, self-affirmations, read the Bible, pray and move towards my goals. *Are you facing a big decision in your life? What fears do you have to overcome and to move forward?*

I encourage you to slow down long enough to think about what YOU REALY WANT!!

Don't be afraid to be different, and do what is outside of your comfort zone.

Don't be afraid to dream big. God would not give you a big dream and not give you the   skills and resources to accomplish it. Trust the process. Keep your spiritual

Make a vision board and add your goals with dates. It's

okay to update the board when needed. Your Goals will change as you reach each one. They will grow and you will be amazed how much you accomplish.

Find what works for you to get through your day when faced with challenges (prayer, meditation or other tools and resources). Know that you will have fear pop up in your mind, but have to courage to push through.

I Decided it was okay to start over at 50, because with God, I decided that is what I wanted to do. Learn what it takes to believe you can achieve anything. It's work, It determination, It's being persistent and consistent.

Make a plan, get into a routine and stick to it.

Be persistent, consistent and never give up!

My final encouragement to you is forgive yourself for past mistakes, know that failing is not the end, but a lesson to better your tomorrow. Continue to keep your awareness open to God guidance and direction. Never give up, be consistent, persistent and trust the process.

About the Author

ಞಲ

SHURVONE WRIGHT, an entrepreneur, owns a small business practice specializing in retirement planning. Using insurance as a foundational component, she helps client families prepare for the future by protecting and preserving what is important to them to leave a legacy and not bills. Her efforts and business acumen have earned recognition with several awards all in one year.

A previous thirty-year healthcare career in nursing provided her an avenue to launch a lifelong commitment of helping others. Shurvone served patients in specialized areas: medical/surgical units, mental health, home health nursing, outpatient clinics. Her last fifteen years were served in managed care as a Pre-Certification Utilization Management Nurse.

Active in her church, she ran the Women's Conference for seven years and assisted in the School of Ministry for five years.

She started a private Facebook women's support group called "Confidence Without Regret" that helps women build confidence and courage on their journey through life.

Shurvone's love of running led her to start a running group. Shurvone has completed over a dozen half marathons, multiple obstacle races, and 10k trail events.

Helping to support local business owners, she has served on the Brentwood Chamber of Commerce Board of Directors, volunteers for community events, and organizes and leads multiple city events.

Married for twenty-five years to Roger Wright, they have four daughters and three grandchildren. Shurvone Wright and her family reside in Brentwood, California.

Contact Shurvone for speaking engagements: ConfidenceWithoutRegret@gmail.com.

A CROWN OF BEAUTY

❧

Meiah Shaun

To bestow on them a crown of beauty instead of ashes, the oil of joy instead of mourning and a garment of praise instead of a spirit of despair."

Isaiah 61:3 (NIV)

No More Bitterness

Did you get laid off from work? Has someone lied on you or betrayed you? Did you get rejected from an opportunity that you pursued? Because of rejection and disappointments, bitterness can fill your heart but do not let it take root. Bitterness can cause you to develop self-hatred, jealousy, envy, and an unloving spirit. You may have gone through many setbacks, disappointments, losses, rejections, which have resulted in emotional distress and trauma. Yet do not become revengeful and pray for your enemies.

In the midst of your crisis, God is turning around your situation. Nothing can deter you because God has not abandoned you. God shall fight for you and all you will need to do is trust in him. Remove all bitterness, and you will no longer be held in bondage.

"No matter how many times you trip them up, God-loyal people don't stay down long; soon they're up on their feet."

Proverbs 24:16 (MSG)

Your setbacks will not prevent you from achieving your God-given destiny. Trust in God's plan for you. Be healed and set free by God's love and divine healing power. You are soaring into your new season of breakthrough.

The Key to Forgivingness

Are you dealing with hurt or betrayal? When you forgive someone, you will receive emotional and spiritual healing. If you have been severely mistreated or abused, you may find it difficult to forgive and will become bitter, angry, fearful, and resentful. You will suffer for holding on to those negative emotions. If you are hurting, you may hurt others with your words and actions. Those emotions are harmful, and you will not be able to grow spiritually. You will not have peace of mind or joy when you are hurting. It is important to break free of these emotions and understand the spiritual root so that you can heal and move forward from your past.

"Cast your cares on the Lord and he will sustain you."

Psalm 55:22 NIV

Initially, it will not feel good to forgive someone who has mistreated you. You are not what others say about you. It is important to eliminate any negative thoughts and feelings you have toward others and yourself. Make the right decision and forgive them and forgive yourself.

It took me years to learn to forgive others. I blamed others for my pain and unhappiness. I was angry, bitter, and I did not trust anyone. And I blamed myself and felt that somehow it may have been my fault. I was insecure about how people perceived me, and I had low self-esteem. In time, God healed my emotions after I recognized my actions and feelings. I had to repent and forgive others and myself. In the beginning, it was painful, but God restored my heart. God's love will help you forgive anyone who has hurt you.

Reject Fear

Fear is the opposite of faith. Reject fear because it will keep you from loving yourself. You have nothing to fear with the Lord on your side. The enemy, Satan, injects fear into your thoughts. Reject the spirit of fear! The Lord loves you, and He wants the best for you.

"There is no fear in love. But perfect love drives out fear."

I John 4:18 (NIV)

The Word of God gives comfort, and it says to fear not. Have faith in the Lord and His plans for your life. When you are operating in fear you will worry, be doubtful, and be depressed. Fear causes you to believe in Satan's lies. The Lord does not give a spirit of fear. He loves you and has given you the strength to overcome any obstacle. Do not give in to the spirit of fear! Cast your cares on the Lord in prayer and confess His Word. You shall have no more restless nights. The Lord will give you peace of mind and rest. Rest in the Lord and His love and peace will heal you.

"When you lie down, you will not be afraid; when you lie down, your sleep will be sweet."

Proverbs 3:24 (NIV)

Receive Your Healing

One night as I was praying to the Lord in the secret place, I asked Him, "Lord, what is the secret You have for me on healing?" He answered, *"Your relationship with Me. There is strength, joy, peace, comfort, understanding, wisdom, and healing, in My word. My word will never return to Me void."* I meditated on His revelation that night and the next several days. I searched through the scriptures to enlighten my understanding of the joy of the Lord, which is my strength.

In the book of Proverbs Chapter 3 it says to trust in the Lord with all your heart and not depend on your own understanding. Studying that passage was the beginning of my inner healing. It was time for me to crack beyond the surface and deal with the spiritual roots.

> *"A happy heart is good medicine and a joyful mind causes healing, but a broken spirit dries up the bones."*
>
> Proverbs 17:22 (AMP)

Almighty God loves you so much that He sent His only Son, Jesus, to sacrifice His own life so that we may live an abundant life. You may have experienced setbacks, disappointments, heartache, abuse, violence, fear, and depression, but just know that our God is a healer and redeemer. Arise, for your time has come. It is a new beginning for you, and your past will no longer deter your life. God has given you hope and a future to soar.

You are worthy of love. When you love yourself, then you will be receptive to another's love. The Lord will sustain you, and you will overcome every setback, disappointment, heartache, and pain. Everything that has been lost and stolen from you, God has restored it back to you. He loves you unconditionally. He has given you an abundant life, and you will overcome any adversity. Let the love of God consume your thoughts, fill your heart, and comfort your soul, and you will begin to see yourself as your Heavenly Father sees you.

"I will praise thee; for I am fearfully and wonderfully made: marvellous are thy works; and that my soul knoweth right well."

Psalm 139:14 (KJV)

Prophecies

Beauty for Ashes

Daughter, I have bestowed upon you a crown of beauty for ashes, the oil of joy instead of mourning and a garment of praise instead of a spirit of despair. You are the sweetest rose in My garden. I uniquely handcrafted you in My image. Let My love fill your heart, where you will remain whole. You shall rise above the flaming arrows from your enemies. I have protected you from the flames, and they shall not touch you. Take your shield of faith, and I will extinguish every flame. Stand firm and you will not be moved. You will fulfill the dreams that I have placed in your heart. Put on your crown and wear your royal apparel as your beauty illuminates the sky. It is time to enter the king's court where your requests are granted. For the plans I have for you are to prosper you for My greater works.

The Oil of Joy and No More Sorrow

Everything you feel you have lost has been restored, My daughters. Do not have any bitterness or regret for anything you have lost or that has been stolen out of your hands. For I am pouring out upon you My spirit of abundant favor and grace. I have not forsaken you, for My promises to you before you were born in your mother's womb still remain and they must be fulfilled for My purpose. I have chosen you, and you are highly favored. Rejoice, for I have redeemed you from the hand of the enemy. You shall have no more sorrow as I shield and cover you. You will soar and arise in this moment. Everything the enemy took from you, I have returned into your hands as a double portion.

Wear Your Garment of Praise

Your joyful noise strums my heart, for I love to hear your praises in the morning, throughout the noonday, and in the evening time. You fill My heart, and I listen to every note as you express unto Me your love and admiration. Put your trust in Me, and I will never let you down. I'm holding you in My arms and will never let you go, for you are the apple of My eye. Your future is brighter than the morning sun. You shall arise and withstand every adversity, for I have shielded you with My splendor. You are My joy, and you shall have abundant life, for you reign in Me. I love to hear your voice, and you are like no other, for I delight in you, My daughter.

Soar in My Army

Daughters of the Most High, I love you dearly. You are in the center of My heart. I am with you day and night. I hear your cries, and I comfort you. I will share My secrets, and you will soar beyond measure with knowledge and wisdom, abundant joy and peace, and prosperity. You have remained hidden, out of the spotlight, but I am causing you to soar higher into a realm of abundant grace. My favor is upon you, so let it radiate. Let it shine on you and from every mountaintop. You will remain far above the status quo, and you shall never be mediocre. You reign in Me, and you are seated with Me in high places, for you shall never come down. You shall mount up on wings like eagles and soar above the seas. I have opened the windows of heaven, and I am pouring out

My blessings into your lap. New inventions will be birthed out of your hands. I am promoting you into new positions for My kingdom agenda to every corner of the earth. You are My nurturers, My ambassadors, My helpmeets, and My messengers in My army. Nothing shall harm you nor forsake you as you soar above every enemy—declare the victory, for it is already won.

Declarations

I am healed. (Isaiah 53:5)

I am renewed in my thoughts and attitudes. (Ephesians 4:23)

I will trust in the Lord with all my heart. (Proverbs 3:5)

I reject the spirit of fear. I have dominion, love, and peace of mind. (2 Timothy 1:7)

The Lord is my helper; I will not be afraid. (Hebrews 13:6)

When I lie down, I will not be afraid, for my sleep will be sweet. (Proverbs 3:24)

I delight myself in the Lord. I shall have the desires of my heart. (Psalm 37:4)

I will be strong and courageous, for the Lord will be with me wherever I go. (Joshua 1:9)

The Lord is my light and my salvation, whom shall I fear? (Psalm 27:1)

The Lord is the strength of my life, of whom shall I be afraid? (Psalm 27:1)

The Lord is my protector, and I will trust in Him. (Psalm 91:2)

No weapon formed against me shall succeed. (Isaiah 54:17)

I am fearfully and wonderfully made. (Psalm 139:13)

I am the apple of God's eye. (Deuteronomy 32:10)

I will succeed, prosper, and remain in good health. (3 John 1:3)

I am virtuous and worth far more than rubies or pearls. (Proverbs 31:10)

New doors are being opened for me. (Matthew 7:7)

For with God nothing shall be impossible for me. (Luke 1:37)

Everything for me will turn out good. (Romans 8:28).

About the Author

❧

MEIAH SHAUN is an author, playwright and prophetic scribe. She writes faith-based messages linking her personal life experiences with spiritual life lessons. Her novel, *Burnt Orange*, is an inspirational coming-of-age novel based on real-life events from her life. Other works include her stage plays, *My First Love* & *A Rich Woman's Party*, published and licensed by HCP Book Publishing.

Meiah is a graduate of LeTourneau University and Touch of God Healing and Deliverance School of Ministry. She studied playwriting at Dallas Theater Center. She is the visionary of *A Crown of Beauty Ministries*, a ministry of healing and deliverance. She is a member of Christ Purpose International Church. She resides in the Dallas, Texas area.

Visit her at https://www.meiahshaun.com.

BOOK REVIEWS

Did you enjoy *Women Who Soar*? Please consider
writing a book review on
Amazon, Barnes & Noble and Goodreads.
Book reviews are important to authors and it only
takes a few minutes to write one.
A review doesn't have to be long. A few short
sentences or
a few words to describe the book works just fine.
Book Recommendations
****

Since you've enjoyed reading *Women Who Soar* will you
help me promote it?
Here's how you can help.

- ✓ Kindly recommend it to books clubs and other readers.
- ✓ Ask your library to carry a copy.
- ✓ Order another copy to give away instead of passing *Women Who Soar* around.
- ✓ Share it on social media as a book recommendation.
- ✓ Invite us to discuss the book either by Skype, Facebook Chat or a visit to your city.

Thank you so much!!

LITERARY WORKS BY PAULETTE HARPER

Non-Fiction Works

That Was Then, This Is Now- If you've recently asked yourself these questions, Paulette Harper's *That Was Then, This is Now* has the answers. Struggling to recover from a broken marriage and disappointed dreams, Paulette Harper gropes for meaning and understanding. And through her searching, God reveals Himself to her in ways she never before imagined possible. By sharing her struggles with transparency, she illustrates how a heart attitude of surrender allows God to use a broken vessel for His ultimate plans of glory.

That Was Then, This is Now, minsters to hurting hearts in every season in life, reminding them that God restores shattered lives, intent on using them for His sovereign purposes.

Completely Whole- it is a "field guide" to help navigate through some of life's most difficult situations. Paulette does not sugar-coat painful dilemmas, but instead helps the reader to recognize God's redemptive plan in even the darkest, most daunting circumstance. This book is inspiring, optimistic, hopeful and encouraging while providing a clear-cut, scriptural blueprint for each reader to follow as they allow the Word and the power of God to transform their pain and restore their lives on their road to becoming "Completely Whole."

Write Now Authors Manual- This manual is your handbook, author's guide, writer's workbook, dictionary, how-to book, and instructional tool to help you become all that you desire in the area of writing. In this manual are your keys to success; it is loaded with terminology used in the industry, recommended books, marketing strategies, and promotional ideas that will help you bring your books to life.

The Scriptures in Color- The Scriptures in Color is a beautifully collection of promises from the Bible. Inside the pages of this book are verses that will help you meditate on His word as you RELAX. UNWIND. BREATHE. Sometimes we need to block out the noise and spend some quiet time with the Lord. So, grab your coloring pencils and let your imagination flow.

Faith for Every Mountain- Are you struggling with

your faith? Are you easily moved by situations beyond your control? If your answer is yes, then this book is for you. It's written to encourage, motivate and challenge you to live a life that pleases God. God's desire is for all His children to have a foundation that is not rocked or shaken by the trials and pitfalls of life. Faith for Every Mountain is one short read and should be added to your arsenal as a believer.

Fiction Works

Living Separate Lives- Four Friends, One Secret and a Weekend that changed their destiny. Four high school friends, Candace Walker, Kaylan Smith, Jordan Tate and Tiffany Thomas have their share of sorry but neither of them realizes how deep the sorry goes. What happens when they agree to meet for a weekend of relaxation in beautiful Napa County?

Secret Places Revealed- Single—and very content—real estate developer Aaron Blackman is determined not to become involved in another relationship. He's experienced enough drama to last a lifetime. The only thing garnering his attention now is his growing business. And he plans to keep it that way. Then Simone Herron waltzes into his life, beautiful and confident. Fighting to keep his promise to himself—

to remain single—he soon discovers that when it comes to love, some promises must be broken. After losing her fiancé in an untimely death, Simone Herron relocates. She desperately needs to put the past behind her and start a new chapter in her life. While love is the farthest thing from her mind, she experiences an attraction to the handsome Aaron Blackman that frightens her. She's built a wall around her heart, but can she find the strength and courage she needs to welcome love again? To do so, she must conquer her fears and allow God to put all of her broken pieces back together.

Anthologies

Arise from The Ashes- Arise from the Ashes, are stories of hope from seven women from all walks of life. These women who have gone through the fire, walked in places that others dare not tread, but women who are not ashamed of their scars and willing to bare it all.

They share their journey of going from trials to triumph and pain to purpose. Arise from the Ashes is filled with inspiration, wisdom and life's lessons from women who have endured personal pain and have come through empowered, encouraged and victorious.

Children

Princess Neveah: Lessons on Self Discovery - Six-year-old Nevaeh wants to be something she already is —a princess. Do you know a little girl that doesn't know she is loved or even beautiful? Do we as parents, grandparents, or guardians reinforce and give our little ones daily affirmation? Princess Nevaeh, Lessons on Self-Discovery covers topics that are important not only to parents but also to our little girls.

Princess Nevaeh, Lessons on Self-Discovery allows caregivers to use this as a tool to affirm the child, build positive dialogue and to encourage self-worth. Find out how Mimi shares with her granddaughter the things that matter most.

Books are available on Amazon & Barnes & Noble.

Made in the USA
Columbia, SC
12 January 2019